Paul Grantham

PRACTICAL APPLICATIONS OF
SOLUTION FOCUSED THERAPY

WORKSHEETS TO USE WITH CLIENTS

CONTENTS

Copyright Information

IMPORTANT – PLEASE READ

All files enclosed in this publication are copyrighted to SDS Seminars Ltd.

They may be printed and used for personal use only or for working with clients conditional on copyright being acknowledged on any reproduced (including printed) version of the worksheets. This may be done without prior permission from SDS Seminars Ltd.

Should the worksheets be *partly* used or *adapted* for use with clients, SDS Seminars Ltd should be approached first and its written permission sought to prevent breach of copyright.

The enclosed files are not to be reproduced or copied for any other purposes without the clear written permission of SDS Seminars Ltd. These include use for purposes of training, education, CPD (Continuing Professional Development); or the intra- and inter- professional development of ideas both within and outside supervision. In any such instances which come to light SDS Seminars Ltd will take decisive legal action.

Introduction

Solution Focused Therapy (SFT) has a strong research and practice background that is currently being practised in a wide range of settings – from child and family work, through severe and enduring mental health, changing health behaviours and palliative care.

Many practitioners however often feel they lack guidance on how to apply solution focused principles in ways that are creative or alternatively would like more structure in how to apply the ideas and principles.

This book is designed to provide that.

It contains 10 exercises in worksheet format that practitioners can use in a variety of settings. It is not designed to replace training in Solution Focused Therapy. It is however designed to facilitate its practise. For those interested in training in Solution Focused approaches have a look at www.skillsdevelopment.co.uk for what is on offer.

Regarding the worksheets:

KEEPING AN EYE ON YOUR PROBLEM is designed to encourage the perception of problem variation with clients. This facilitates the client to perceive their situation as "fluid" (rather than "stuck") which in turn enables both client and practitioner to identify "exceptions"

DOING THE PROBLEM IN DETAIL is a semi-paradoxical exercise. Ostensibly it encourages the client to immerse themselves in their problem. In practice however it enables the client to identify the boundaries to their problem – including when it is absent – and thus identify exceptions and what they do/might do to enhance these.

DO YOUR PROBLEM DIFFERENTLY uses Bill O'Hanlon's concept of Contextual Pattern Intervention. In plain language, this is the idea that problems are often maintained by their ritual and context and that if the client disturbs this ritual and context, the problem becomes much weaker and may even disappear.

WALKING THROUGH A GALE Most non-systemic therapies take a linear approach to personal and behaviour change. Solution Focused Therapy is a rare exception. It recognises that "what works" for the client is often not necessarily direct or obvious or alternatively is so simple, that everyone ignores it. This worksheet helps clients to recognise both that direct confrontation is not necessarily always the best approach, plus it encourages the development of creative solutions.

YOU'RE NOT A D*CKHEAD Anyone who has ever worked with an interpreter will know that the opportunities for miscommunication are numerous. Every time a practitioner translates what a client says into their own jargon or language, he/she is prone to creating the same dangers. This worksheet was developed as a hybrid of SFT ACT and CBT when working with young offenders. It uses the clients' own language for regarding their NATs and Cognitive Assumptions, encourages them to change their relationship with such thoughts (Cognitive Defusion in ACT terms) and uses the clients' often natural antagonistic attitudes as a resource as a way of creating change.

PLAYING WITH VOICES attempts a similar approach to the previous worksheet except it more consciously uses Cognitive Defusion Techniques.

DOING THE SOLUTION OPTIMALLY uses the Solution Focused strategy of the Relationship Question in a creative way. We know that asking clients to perceive change from a 3rd Party perspective is often easier for them to do than from a 1st party perspective ("What would your partner say has changed about you?" vs "What's changed about you?"). This worksheet makes the client their own 3rd Party whilst also facilitating "success behaviour"

IT'S OK TO FAKE IT Pretence is a strategy, extensively used by human beings as a way of both learning and testing out. In children it is called "play" and adults often use it whilst they are "consciously incompetent" but trying to develop "conscious competence". Pretence also helps many clients overcome the obstacle of the negative belief that "I can't change". This worksheet explicitly uses the strategy of pretence to enable clients to both discover how they've effectively used it in the past as well as how they might use it constructively in the future.

FIRST AID KIT We know that thinking naturally becomes rigid and "tunnel visioned" when we are in crisis. Hence, eliciting strategies that have been useful in the past (in time of crisis) or creatively identifying things we might be able to use, is much easier in advance. This worksheet is a simple strategy to enable clients to achieve that.

EXPERIMENTS Clients, being the resourceful people they are, have typically used a number of ways to try and address their problem before they seek help. These "experiments" work with varying degrees of success. Just because they haven't fully produced the result the client wanted, doesn't mean they have no value at all. This worksheet encourages clients to both identify what they have done to tackle their problem and to "tease out" the strengths that different strategies might offer.

Paul Grantham

Consultant Clinical Psychologist

KEEPING AN EYE ON YOUR PROBLEM

Choose a set time in the day that's best for you to rate what your problem is like. Try to make sure it's roughly the same time each day.

When you rate what your problem is AT THAT MOMENT remember that:

'0' = The worst it could ever possibly be. The worst catastrophe possible.

'10' = The best things could ever be with your problem totally gone.

List the things each day YOU think make it higher or lower

For today, rate yourself NOW.

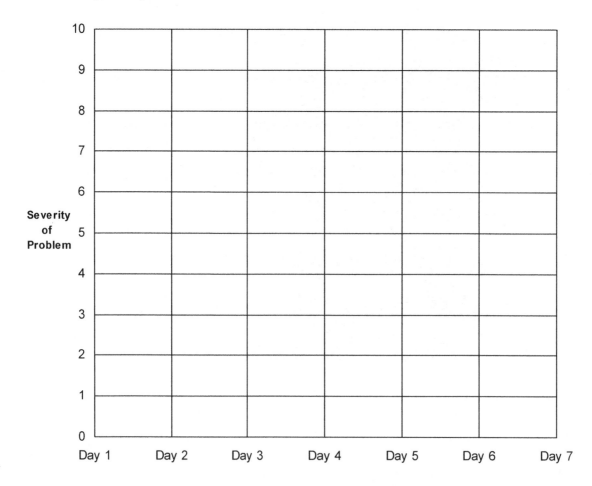

Day 1

_____
_____
_____
_____

Day 2

_____
_____
_____
_____

Day 3

_____
_____
_____
_____

Day 4

_____
_____
_____
_____

Day 5

_____
_____
_____
_____

Day 6

_____
_____
_____
_____

Day 7

_____
_____
_____
_____

Remember to bring your completed work sheet to your next appointment

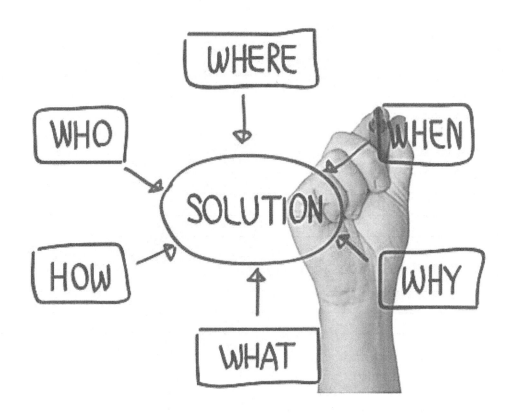

DOING THE PROBLEM IN DETAIL

We would like you to study the problem you have in more detail and to keep a close eye on yourself and other people when you are "doing" this problem. The closer you look at the problem and the more detailed your description, the better.

1. When does the problem usually occur?

_____

_____

_____

_____

2. When does the problem usually NOT occur?

_____

_____

_____

_____

3. Where does the problem usually occur?

_____

_____

_____

_____

_____

4. Where does the problem usually NOT occur?

_____

_____

_____

_____

_____

5. What else is always around when the problem occurs/doesn't occur (e.g. people, clothing you're wearing, what you're thinking)

_____

_____

_____

_____

_____

6. What's the first hint you get that the problem is starting?

_____

_____

_____

_____

_____

_____

7. How do you respond to that?

_____

_____

_____

_____

_____

8. If there are other people around at this time how do they respond to this?

_____

_____

_____

_____

_____

9. What happens next?

_____

_____

_____

_____

_____

10. How do you know that the problem is about to finish?

_____

_____

_____

_____

_____

11. How do you know when the problem has finished?

_____

_____

_____

_____

_____

DO YOUR PROBLEM DIFFERENTLY

We would like you to try something which may sound slightly strange but which some people have found useful.

We don't want you to change anything about your problem at the moment. However, we would like you to _experiment_ in how you actually do your problem.

Look at the list of things/conditions below. Try changing each of these, _one at a time._ Concentrate on only changing the one element at a time and make sure that everything else is kept the same.

1. How could you change the timing of when the problem happens?

_____

_____

_____

2. How could you change what you do before the problem starts?

_____

_____

_____

3. How could you change what you do after the problem happens?

_____

_____

_____

_____

4. How could you change what others do before/during or after?

_____

_____

_____

_____

5. How could you change what clothes you wear?

_____

_____

_____

_____

6. **How could you change where you experience the problem?**

_____

_____

_____

_____

7. **How could you change how you move/don't move whilst doing your problem?**

_____

_____

_____

_____

8. **How could you change any other typical actions/aspects of the problem?**

_____

_____

_____

_____

WALKING THROUGH A GALE

COMPUTER GAME

Imagine that you are the person in the screen-shot from the computer game below.

You are at one end of the street and you have to get to the top of the street.

There is a fierce gale blowing down the street.

If you just directly face the wind and walk up the street, it will push you back and you will give up with exhaustion.

The only way to do it is slowly edge your way across to the other pavement and up to the opening on the left. This is the entrance to a corridor that will take you up the street and to safety.

1. If the things stopping you changing your life are like the gale "pushing you back", what are they?

_____

_____

_____

_____

2. If you had to face these things head on, what would happen? If you have tried this approach in the past, what has happened?

_____

_____

_____

_____

3. If you were to just ignore these things that push you back, what would happen?

_____

_____

_____

_____

4. In the computer game what sorts of things could you do that might help to get across to the opening of the corridor?

_____

_____

_____

_____

5. Regarding your problem what sorts of things could you do that might make it easier to overcome your problem without directly facing the things you are up against?

_____

_____

_____

_____

YOU ARE NOT A D*CKHEAD!

Although you often tell yourself you're d*ckhead for the situations you've got yourself into, you're not.

Your negative thinking is often d*ckhead-like however. But the two aren't the same.

Below are some questions that people like yourself have sometimes found helpful in remembering that.

1. **Give your negative thinking a name.** *(You can call it d*ckhead if you want, but you might find a better name for it. Just remember that this is what you'll be calling it from now on.)*

_____

2. **Why did you give your negative thinking this name?**

_____

_____

3. **What are eight words you would use to describe your negative thinking to a friend?**

1. _____   2. _____

3. _____   4. _____

5. _____   6. _____

7. _____   8. _____

4. Is your negative thinking male, female, or asexual?

_____

5. What does he/she/it look like?

   Describe your negative thinking with words or a picture.

_____

_____

_____

_____

_____

_____

A PICTURE OF MY NEGATIVE THINKING

6. **Give an example (or several examples) of how your negative thinking tricked you into doing something that created problems for you**

_____

_____

_____

7. **If you wanted to give your negative thinking a piece of your mind and tell it what you think of it, what would you say?**

_____

_____

_____

PLAYING WITH VOICES

Sometimes our thinking is very negative or it gets us into trouble. You can't always stop the negative thoughts but you could try experimenting trying to change them in some way.
Some of the things below may look a little strange but people like yourself have sometimes found them helpful. Try them out and find out what is helpful or unhelpful.

1. Write down a thought that is negative or often gets you into trouble

_____

_____

_____

2. Repeat the thought three times in fast motion. Then do it again and again so that it sounds like The Crazy Frog. What's that like?

_____

_____

_____

_____

3. Repeat the thought three times VERY slowly indeed like a slurred drunk. What's that like?

_____

_____

_____

4. Repeatedly shout the thought as loud as you can. What's that like?

_____

_____

_____

5. Whisper the thought three times so you barely hear it. What's that like?

_____

_____

_____

6. Choose your favourite TV or film personality and repeatedly say the thought in that voice.

_____

_____

_____

7. State the thought once in the tone and volume you usually hear it.

_____

_____

_____

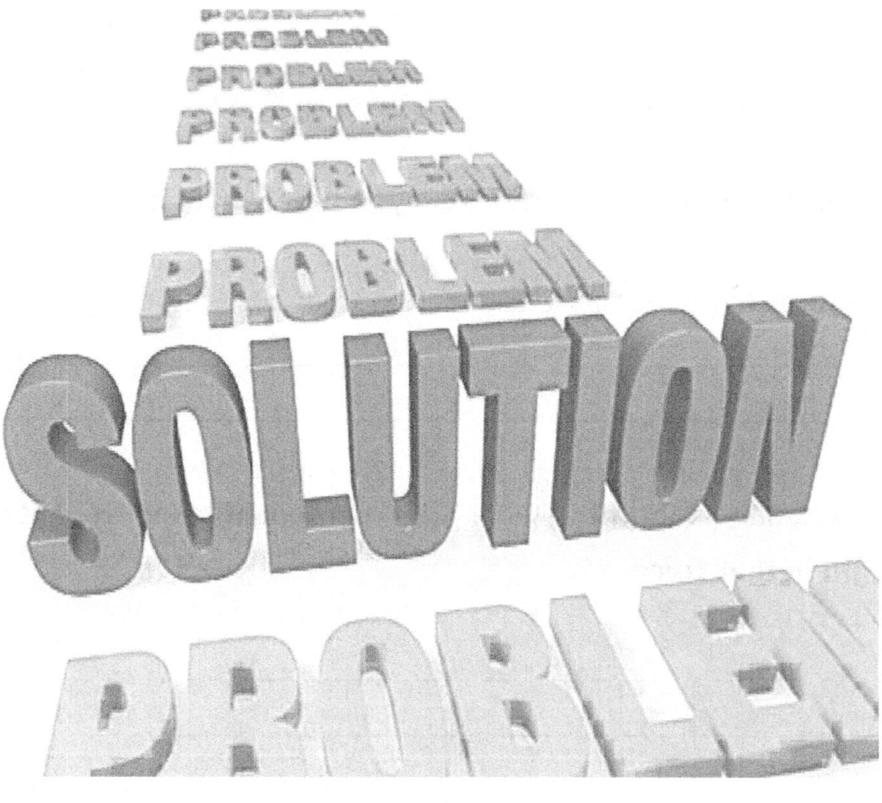
PROBLEM
PROBLEM
PROBLEM
PROBLEM
PROBLEM
SOLUTION

DOING THE SOLUTION OPTIMALLY

On a scale of 0 – 10 (where '0' is being a total disaster and '10' is totally solving your problem) what number would you currently give yourself?

1	2	3	4	5	6	7	8	9	10

Imagine you are teaching someone else how to move from your current No. to the next one up (e.g. a '1' to a '2' or a '7' to an '8').

What would you advise them to do?

What should they wear that would make it easier for them?

_____

_____

_____

At what time of day should they best do it?

_____

_____

_____

_____

What would be the easiest way for them to get started?

_____

_____

_____

_____

How would they keep it going?

_____

_____

_____

_____

Where would be the easiest place to be doing it?

_____

_____

_____

What should they actually do when they are doing this which would make it easier for them? Should they be sitting, standing, talking, being silent….what?

_____

_____

_____

_____

_____

IT'S OK TO FAKE IT

Most things we do in life for the first time seem strange and artificial. They feel that they are "not me" or uncomfortable, fake or odd.

We want to encourage you to experiment with different fake behaviour as many people like you have often found it useful.

1. **List five things that you have had to do for the first time in your life at some point and cast your mind back to what it felt like at the time.**

   Rate how "normal"/comfortable each felt the first time you did them where '10' is totally normal and natural and '0' is totally strange, alien or uncomfortable.

	0	1	2	3	4	5	6	7	8	9	10
1.											
2.											
3.											
4.											
5.											

2. **List the same five things again below and rate them in terms of how "normal"/comfortable they feel NOW.**

	0	1	2	3	4	5	6	7	8	9	10
1.											
2.											
3.											
4.											
5.											

3. **What did you do that helped you to increase your score on one or more of these?**

4. Rate yourself NOW on a scale of 0 – 10,

where '0' is the worst things could ever possibly be for me, the worst catastrophe possible and '10' is the best things could ever be with your problem totally gone.

My Rating =

5. Try one of the following over the next week:

a) Pretend for one hour a day to be one number higher in your rating. Fake it. Remember, you're just trying it out like you would try on a new pair of shoes.

What did you do to pretend?

_____

_____

_____

_____

What were the pros and cons of it?

_____

_____

_____

_____

What surprised you the most about it?

_____

_____

_____

_____

b) Tell some person/people you know well that you're going to pretend to be one number higher on one day during the next week, but you're not going to tell them which day.

Their job is to guess.

Who guessed correctly?

_____

_____

_____

_____

How did they know?

_____

_____

_____

_____

What was their attitude towards your faking it?

_____

_____

_____

_____

What surprised you the most about their reaction/feedback?

_____

_____

_____

_____

FIRST AID KIT

You know how it's useful to have a first aid kit at home in case of colds, cuts or bruises.
The same is true when problems crop up. It's useful to have a range of things you know might be helpful.
Fill in the list below and tape it somewhere you can find it easily… just like a first aid kit.

List 10 or more things that you could do that would be helpful if your problem starts to cause you trouble. These could be things that you found useful in the past, things that other people suggested, or even things that have crossed your mind MIGHT work even though you've never tried them yet.

1. _____

2. _____

3. _____

4. _____

5. _____

6. _____

7. _____

8. _____

9. _____

10. _____

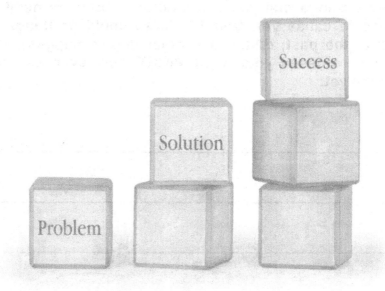

EXPERIMENTS

If we have had a problem for a while we often try to deal with it in a number of different ways. This is a bit like conducting experiments. Some of these experiments produce better results than others. It is very easy to forget about the things we've tried out in the past. Now is a good time to try and remember them.

Write down at least five ways that you have tried to deal with your problem.

These will be your 5 experiments. Give each of them a name and answer the following questions.

Experiment 1

_____

_____

Where did you get the idea for experiment 1?

_____

_____

_____

_____

What did you like about this experiment?

_____

_____

_____

_____

What were its disadvantages?

_____

_____

_____

_____

What did you learn from this experiment?

_____

_____

_____

_____

Experiment 2

_____

_____

Where did you get the idea for experiment 2?

_____

_____

_____

_____

What did you like about this experiment?

_____

_____

_____

_____

What were its disadvantages?

_____

_____

_____

_____

What did you learn from this experiment?

_____

_____

_____

_____

Experiment 3

_____
_____

Where did you get the idea for experiment 3?

_____
_____
_____
_____

What did you like about this experiment?

_____
_____
_____
_____

What were its disadvantages?

_____
_____
_____
_____

What did you learn from this experiment?

_____
_____
_____
_____

Experiment 4

_____

_____

Where did you get the idea for experiment 4?

_____

_____

_____

_____

What did you like about this experiment?

_____

_____

_____

_____

What were its disadvantages?

_____

_____

_____

_____

What did you learn from this experiment?

_____

_____

_____

_____

Experiment 5

_____

_____

Where did you get the idea for experiment 5?

_____

_____

_____

_____

What did you like about this experiment?

_____

_____

_____

_____

What were its disadvantages?

_____

_____

_____

_____

What did you learn from this experiment?

_____

_____

_____

_____

Recommended Materials:

Reading:

Bannink F. (2015) 101 Solution-Focused Questions for Help with Trauma; 101 Solution-Focused Questions for Help with Anxiety; 101 Solution-Focused Questions for Help with Depression

Bliss E. V. and Edmonds G. (2007). *A self-determined future and Asperger syndrome: solution focused approaches*. London: Jessica Kingsley Publishers

De Shazer S. (1988) Clues: Investigating Solutions in Brief Therapy W.W. Norton

De Shazer S., Dolan Y., Korman H., Trepper T., McCollum E.E. & Berg I.K. (2005). More than Miracles. Haworth Press.

Jackson P. & McKergow M. (2002). The solutions focus, the SIMPLE way to positive change. Nicholas Brealy Publishing.

Lipchik E. (2002). Beyond Technique In Solution-Focused Therapy. Working With Emotions And The Therapeutic Relationship. Guilford Publications

O'Connell B. (2012) Solution-Focused Therapy (Brief Therapies series). Sage

Quick E.K. (2016) Core Competencies in the Solution-Focused and Strategic Therapies: Becoming a Highly Competent Solution-Focused and Strategic Therapist (Core Competencies in Psychotherapy Series)

Rae T. (2016) The Essential Guide to Solution Focused Brief Therapy (SFBT) with Young People (Hinton House Essential Guides)

Ratner H., George E. (2012) Solution Focused Brief Therapy (100 Key Points)

Visser C.F. & Schlundt Bodien G. (2008). Paden naar oplossingen. De kracht van oplossingsgericht werken. JustInTimeBooks.

http://solworld.ning.com/profiles/blogs/2102269:BlogPost:5384

Viewing:

All available from www.psychotherapydvds.com

"I'd Hear Laughter": Finding Solutions for the Family - 2 CPD Hours

Children and teenagers are all too often the scapegoat to a family's troubles and the impetus for a family to enter therapy. In this video, Insoo Kim Berg shows us how to help a family come together as a whole to build on their strengths and collaborate on solutions.

Addressing a Client's Relationship with Drink (Solution Focused Live Case Consultation) 2 CPD Hours

Solution Focused Therapy (SFT) offers a unique strengths oriented approach to behaviour and attitude change based on a social constructionist philosophy. Its assumption of constant change, preexisting success and resources combined with a focus on what a problem free future would consist of, ensures a positive therapeutic approach.

Irreconcilable Differences: A Solution-Focused Approach to Marital Therapy - 2 CPD Hours

Insoo Kim Berg's unique style and unwavering optimism comes to life in this demonstration of Solution-Focused Brief Therapy.

Solution Focused Therapy in Family Problems (Solution Focused Live Case Consultation) - 2 CPD Hours

Solution Focused Therapy (SFT) offers a unique strengths oriented approach to behaviour and attitude change based on a social constructionist philosophy. Its assumption of constant change, preexisting success and resources combined with a focus on what a problem free future would consist of, ensures a positive therapeutic approach.

Solution-Focused Child Therapy - 2 CPD Hours

Watch Solution-Focused child therapist John J. Murphy in an actual counselling session with two boys and their mother.

Solution-Focused Therapy - 2 CPD Hours

Watch Insoo Kim Berg masterfully demonstrate Solution-Focused Therapy in an actual therapy session in this 3-part video. What a treat to see this legendary therapist in action!

Solution-Oriented Family Therapy - 2 CPD Hours

Watch Bill O'Hanlon passionately discuss and demonstrate his innovative approach in this three-part video, which includes an actual therapy session with an intriguing, non-traditional family.

The Miracle Question & Its Use in Anger Management - 1 CPD Hour

A practical video demonstration of this innovative psychological intervention for use with clients, combined with comprehensive comments and reflections from Paul Grantham, Consultant Clinical Psychologist.

All available from www.psychotherapydvds.com

Further Training:

Certificate In Resource Based Therapies (3 modules/5 days)

 *Approved by the British Psychological Society for the purposes of Continuing Professional Development (CPD).*

The Certificate in Resource Based Therapies (RBT) Course consists of 3 modules / 5 training days that can be booked together or separately.

3 Modules of the Certificate in Resource Based Therapies:

- Positive Therapy

- Motivational Interviewing & Beyond (2 day course)

- Solution Focused Brief Therapy (2 day course)

The order, in which delegates attend the courses, is flexible.

Delegates who attend one or more days will be awarded with a Certificate of Attendance (on the day).

As an additional option delegates can take an assessment (comprising of additional reading and an online test) – successful completion of which will result in obtaining a Certificate of Assessed Academic Competence with 30 CPD hours.

For more information visit: www.skillsdevelopment.co.uk

Made in the USA
Las Vegas, NV
21 December 2020